Jena Rose Creative
www.jenarosecreative.com
Instagram: @jenaroseIII

© 2021 Jena Rose

Published 2021

Cover design and illustrations by Lilly Prinz
Book design by Brynn Woodley

All Rights Reserved. This book or any portion there of may not be reproduced or used in any manner whatsoever without the express written permission of the author except for the use of brief quotations in a book review.

―――

The author of this book does not dispense medical advice or prescribe the use of any technique as a form of treatment for physical, emotional or medical problems without the advice of a physician, either directly or indirectly. The intent of the author is only to offer information of a general nature to help you on your journey for emotional, physical and spiritual well being. In the event you use any of the information for yourself, the author and the publisher assume no responsibility for your actions.

Closer to Love is a collection of poetry, quotes and short stories that are split into five chapters about remembering love and coming home to your heart.

Closer to Love is an activation and transmission in written form in hopes that you may remember who you are on a multi-dimensional, soul level. As you read through this you may find yourself becoming conscious in all areas of your life that need healing, and wanting to shed layers of what no longer serves you so you may become closer to your true being, *so you may rise.*

I hope this book inspires you to go within, to feel some love towards yourself and others and to see the light you truly are.

Also by **Jena Rose**

———

Entangled by Nature

CLOSER TO LOVE

Jena Rose

May you be activated
May this be your reminder
May you continue to
Remember

CONTENTS

Prelude i

Activating 1

Remembering 73

Becoming 125

Rising 155

Afterword 235

Acknowledgments 236

About the Author 237

Author's Note 239

Prelude

I lost who I was, trying to fit in with this world, the programming. I became what people expected of me, a part of the matrix. I became separated from myself. Rather than following my soul, I had forgotten who I was and my purpose in this life. I had lost touch with my inner child. Until I remembered.

Over time, the crumbling started taking place. The more I expanded my consciousness, healed myself and went inward, the more I started to remember who I was. My core. My soul. Things started to make more sense. Everything that wasn't me, started falling away. The veil was lifted from my minds eye. The illusion of this world was made clear to me. I saw how everything is connected. I have grown to understand life on a much deeper level.

It was love that reminded me. Love healed my wounds and brought me closer to myself and maybe that's one of the things we are supposed to learn in this life. The sense of losing self, just so you can evolve and rediscover yourself all over again.

I hope that after you read this that
you will feel closer to yourself and

Closer to Love.

CLOSER TO LOVE

My wish for everyone
is that the they never let their hearts harden
That they can feel safe to be seen
and let their hearts soften
To see through the eyes of love more
and to be in touch with their soul

To remember who they are
— That's it

CLOSER TO LOVE

I am a woman of fire
gentle
fierce
and warm

In my heart there is
a burning passion for this world

My goal is to ignite a fiery path
to be a beacon
shining out light and love
to and for everyone

You are l o v e

Divine energy circulates through you

You are valued and supported by the higher angelic realms

— *Remember*

Activating

Surrender: Deep healing is taking place

CLOSER TO LOVE

What if falling apart is just another way to describe what coming together feels like?

We fall apart and come back together. Fall apart and come back together. Growing, evolving and becoming stronger each time. I think the goal of this is to always work towards our highest good and evolution for growth. There are always lessons to be learned but the ones we don't pass we keep getting the same curve ball thrown at us over and over again until we can recognize the pattern and rise above. To transcend.

Sometimes I wonder if life is about losing a sense of self only to find it all over again. People are placed into our lives to teach us lessons and help us to remember who we are. What we do and don't like, what resonates with us and what doesn't. To help us remember and recall lost fragments of our soul. Everything in this life is connected and there is something to be learned from everything that all contributes to our path in this life.

CLOSER TO LOVE

As I lay and stare into the night sky
the moon speaks to me
She reminds me that she has a shadow too
but it doesn't make her any less beautiful
and even though she gets consumed
by the darkness at times
that she is still appreciated

and still finds a way to
Shine

— O —

CLOSER TO LOVE

"Can you sit with the discomfort
of what you have yet to let go of?"

CLOSER TO LOVE

As many timelines folded out in front of me
I realized that maybe I wasn't asking myself
the right questions before

Our inner truth isn't always where we think we will find it

CLOSER TO LOVE

As much as you may try
    you can not run
or hide
    from what's
        inside

CLOSER TO LOVE

The

      m o o n

always shines her

      l i g h t

  on the things

I wish to forget

— shadow work

CLOSER TO LOVE

Can you sit with yourself and listen to your thoughts as they come? Can you allow your feelings to exist instead of allowing them to drive your actions right now?

Recognize them, hear them and let them pass by like clouds.

Can you observe your life as it is happening and accept your current life situation without self judgment, criticism or struggle?

Notice your thoughts, hear these parts of yourself and let them flow.

Can you sit with yourself without necessarily agreeing or disagreeing with what comes up, but remaining neutral?

Feel it in your heart, open with love. Notice your breath. Feel and connect to it with your body.

Be the witness to yourself, the observer, the ever present awareness.

CLOSER TO LOVE

Within the darkness

you will find more of yourself

———

CLOSER TO LOVE

At what point in my journey
did I grow to hate myself?

— *Therapy sessions with self*

CLOSER TO LOVE

Lately

    the moon

        has been

            casting shadows

                over me

CLOSER TO LOVE

At what point in my journey
did I grow to distrust myself and my intuition?

From now on I will trust myself
and stop seeking answers from without
and start seeking answers from within

I will trust that every choice I make
is always the right one
even if things don't work out the way I plan

That the choice was still the right one
because whatever lesson it'll bring
will have been a lesson that was needed to be learned

How could anything ever be a mistake
if you have learned something?

CLOSER TO LOVE

> We need darkness
> in order to shine
>
> Without the night sky
> we wouldn't have the stars

CLOSER TO LOVE

I've noticed that after I express a certain feeling
or I cry in front of others
whether it was over something sad
or joyful

I apologize

As if to feel
is wrong

At what point did this happen?

— *Something that needs more addressing*

CLOSER TO LOVE

Why do I still try to understand things

that I possibly can't know?

CLOSER TO LOVE

Although

    I embrace

        change

            I sometimes

        resist what is

good for me

CLOSER TO LOVE

I've been tricked
too many times

to know the truth
from a lie

CLOSER TO LOVE

Do you ever reflect on your past
and wonder why you ever thought
something was good for you?

— *Me too*

CLOSER TO LOVE

You know
you haven't
always had
it good

when
your heart
gets suspicious

of a good thing

CLOSER TO LOVE

> The ghosts
>
> of my past
>
> come to
>
> haunt me
>
> often

CLOSER TO LOVE

Feelings

    rise up

        inside of me

            like the tide

        and just like the waves

      that come and go

or break upon the sand

            so do my emotions

        Consuming me

        Flooding me

Crashing over me

— Eb and flow —

CLOSER TO LOVE

It feels like everything is unwinding
in slow motion

Everything has just slowed down
to a smooth rhythm of something

unfamiliar

CLOSER TO LOVE

That feeling
when you aren't

good — or — bad

but somewhere in between

CLOSER TO LOVE

It's okay
to want time alone

Even the moon
and sun have days
that they want to

disappear

CLOSER TO LOVE

>When you're feeling low
>protect your energy
>because toxic/unhealthy people
>will try to take advantage
>of a vulnerable situation
>
>Protect yourself

CLOSER TO LOVE

Lean

    into

        the

    unknown

To

    learn

        more

            about

    yourself

CLOSER TO LOVE

The more I learn

The more I question

...

CLOSER TO LOVE

He broke her heart

    and shattered her world

but through being broken

    she found more of herself

CLOSER TO LOVE

I thought I was the one

who lost you

but you were the one who

let me go

CLOSER TO LOVE

Always be grateful
for what you have

You never know
how long you'll have it for

CLOSER TO LOVE

You might lose your way
but it's never too late
to come back home to

who you are

CLOSER TO LOVE

If you're always seeking forgiveness

where in your life
are you not forgiving yourself?

CLOSER TO LOVE

Sometimes we have to accept
that we just don't mean the same thing
to some people as they mean to us

Some people will not love you
the way you love them
Don't internalize this
as if you aren't capable of love
or that you don't deserve love

Maybe they aren't capable of loving you
the way you need
Maybe they are closed off inside
Maybe you just aren't a good fit
and the universe is potentially saving you from something

All we can do is love
We can't determine whether others will appreciate it
but just know

your love is enough

CLOSER TO LOVE

If it makes you anxious and fearful
then is it really love?

CLOSER TO LOVE

If something doesn't work out a certain way, that is God guiding you back onto something better.

It didn't work out because it wasn't meant to and there is something better for you. Even if that is hard to believe right now. Keep chasing after what you desire and believe that you deserve the highest love. I know it gets hard sometimes but it'll pass. The pain is necessary and a part of the process.

Try to sit and maintain inner peace through the midst of it all. Take one day at a time and focus on the things you still have to be grateful for.

CLOSER TO LOVE

Affirm:

When everything feels like it's falling apart
I will choose to believe that it's everything falling into place

CLOSER TO LOVE

One of the best gifts you could give someone
is the comfortability to be themselves

so that they may feel

s

  e

    e

      n

CLOSER TO LOVE

When we remove ourselves
from expected outcomes
and attachments
we remove suffering

Self inflicting suffering
comes from expectations

Have a desire and then release it

Surrender your attachment
in order to attain a happier and more full life

CLOSER TO LOVE

Believe in the unseen

Believe that everything is working out for your highest good

Believe in the miracles that are coming your way

Wake up each day thinking that something magnificent can happen

You won't ever regret having a positive mindset

CLOSER TO LOVE

Everything is aligning

trust in the divine timing

CLOSER TO LOVE

Running away from the pain
only causes more of it

When you run away from the pain
you are only suppressing your own healing

— Acknowledge your feelings

CLOSER TO LOVE

Whenever I was rejected in the past
I always took it as if there was something wrong with me

But this was also because I didn't value my worth
So because I didn't see or value my own worth
I unconsciously attracted and sought out those
who also didn't see or value my worth
and there is also a strong chance that those same people
also didn't value themselves

Then, during one of my meditations this realization hit:

People can only know you as much as they know themselves
People can only understand you as much as they understand themselves
People can only value you as much as they value themselves
People can only meet you as deep as they have met themselves
People can only love you as much as they love themselves
and so on

Mmm ... Let that sink in deeply for a moment ...

CLOSER TO LOVE

People can only meet you wherever they are at
with their own sacred journey

So whenever you're feeling like people don't see you
value you or love you
maybe they haven't met themselves that deeply

Which means if they can't give that to themselves
they won't be able to give that to you either

If they can't give these needs to themselves
we can't expect them to give it to us or others

Send them love and encouragement
for their healing, love and self discovery

CLOSER TO LOVE

Instead of running away from your feelings

Run right towards them

No matter how unpleasant they are

That is where your answers lie

Within yourself

CLOSER TO LOVE

You will grow disappointed
if you seek for the truth and answers
in anything or anyone that is outside of yourself

CLOSER TO LOVE

Your emotions are safe
it is safe to feel
and sometimes
when you address a feeling
or an emotion that is unpleasant
it can feel like removing
shards of glass or a sliver
it can be painful at first

But ... the key to your own inner F r E e D o M
is through your own healing

You hold the keys to your own freedom
no one else does

Please don't imprison yourself
you are liberated
you are F r E e

within and without

CLOSER TO LOVE

Allowing yourself to feel
softens you ...

... It's how the love gets in

CLOSER TO LOVE

We know our love is deserving and what it feels like for someone to think it isn't. We understand that feeling of being rejected, so we love anyway and see beyond the flaws of others. We all want to be loved and accepted. Although sometimes our definition of love doesn't match the definition of what love means to others. There may be times that it feels like others don't want us, but that isn't a time to internalize it and believe there is something wrong with who we are or that we aren't capable of being loved. Maybe that's Gods way of guiding us more within, to love ourselves a little more.

So if someone rejects your love, don't internalize that as if you aren't worthy. Maybe they just don't know how to love themselves in the way that you are capable of. People can only love us as much as they love themselves. Just like, people can only meet us as deep as they have met themselves. Our energy isn't a match for everyone and that doesn't mean you are undeserving of anything wonderful.

You are worthy of all things
loving and
beautiful

CLOSER TO LOVE

Don't sacrifice your worth to people
that don't value you or your feelings

CLOSER TO LOVE

People's limited perception of me
is not my responsibility

— *Repeat*

CLOSER TO LOVE

Don't keep coming back
to something you don't like

Walk away from what doesn't
resonate with you

Don't keep repeating the same timeline

CLOSER TO LOVE

You shouldn't deny
your own self worth

even if others can't see it

CLOSER TO LOVE

Don't worry

        the right people

will see your

        m a g i c

CLOSER TO LOVE

If you keep asking yourself the same questions over and over
you already know the answers deep down

Your intuition knows its shit

Stop second guessing yourself and resisting the change
Sometimes you have to get out of your own way
Don't let your ego be what stands between you
and the answers in which you seek

CLOSER TO LOVE

If something doesn't work out the way you plan
it's because it wasn't meant to work out
Source / God could potentially be saving you from
something.

Everything happens for a reason

Look more closely

CLOSER TO LOVE

Sometimes we can't change the things
that are going on around us
but we can change the way we choose to perceive it
or subscribe to it

CLOSER TO LOVE

Whatever is meant to be
a path will be cleared for me —

CLOSER TO LOVE

When life gets a little blurry
adjust your focus

You know those moments
when it feels like nothing
but bad things are happening?

In those moments
it's an invitation for us to look closer
To go within and examine our situations

Whenever I'm faced off with something difficult
these are some of the questions I ask myself:

What is something good that can come from this?
How does this serve my highest self?
What can I learn from this?

When a difficult situation presents itself to you
how do you choose to look at it?

Do you see life as a continual struggle?

Or do you accept what is and try and make the best of it?

CLOSER TO LOVE

It's normal to get down from time to time
but it's important that we don't allow ourselves to get
trapped there

This is real life

Things aren't good all the time
but it's how we choose to make it that counts

Try and find a way to make the "bad times" more fun

CLOSER TO LOVE

If you keep making
the same mistakes
over and over

You'll only delay
your own healing
growth and ascension

CLOSER TO LOVE

Affirm:

Every struggle I face can be used for the greater good
to inspire myself and those around me

Every struggle I face gives me the opportunity to grow
and love myself more

Every struggle I face expands my soul
and brings me closer to myself
to source and closer to love

— and so it is —

CLOSER TO LOVE

When pain comes knocking at my door
my initial response is to put my walls up
and harden/close off my heart

I'm used to doing this per survival/instinct

But it takes far more strength
to respond with love in these situations
and what I've learned is that you can keep your heart soft
while processing through the pain
while healing

You don't have to lose yourself

CLOSER TO LOVE

Affirm:

I remain grounded
as my troubles
wash over me

CLOSER TO LOVE

If you are feeling out of alignment with a person, experience or job, don't be afraid to take a step back and acknowledge what you are feeling. Listen to the energies that are being put into your field. This is your intuition guiding you toward your truth. Trust your feelings and emotions no matter what they are. Even if they don't make sense to you at first — that will come later. We have been programmed to not be able to trust ourselves or rely on ourselves, but you have all the answers inside you.

— *Trust the inner knowing*

CLOSER TO LOVE

Don't drain your energy
by holding onto things
that aren't meant to be

You'll find
that when something is meant to be
it won't feel forced
It'll happen almost casually
or effortlessly

Things will seamlessly fall together
It won't feel like friction
or like two magnets being pushed together

Things will fall into place
Like the rain
and how easily it falls
from the clouds

Like a shooting star
reaching across the sky
or a flower
blooming in spring

CLOSER TO LOVE

In order for more good things
to come your way

You need to be willing to let go
of what no longer deserves
to take up

s

p

a

c

e

in your life

CLOSER TO LOVE

A prayer for your heart

———

God, source, angels, spirit guides and all energy loving and positive. Please come in and heal my heart. Mend these wounds that never seem to heal. Help me to surrender and let go. Help me to accept all that is. Mend the parts of me that still feel empty. Please, guide me within and help me feel whole again.

CLOSER TO LOVE

So many people confuse vulnerability for weakness
but through vulnerability is how we connect to others

It's where the love gets in

Although our stories may be different
we are all going through this journey of life together

CLOSER TO LOVE

> Vulnerability shatters
> the illusion of perfection
>
> life is messy
> and no one ever
> has it all together

CLOSER TO LOVE

You're not always going to know the path thats unfolding. The only way to find out, is to take conscious action. Step out in faith and the net will appear. Yes, doors will open and close along the way, but everything will guide you back to your purpose, back to your highest good. Believe that everything serves you and that there is something to be gained from everything. Remember, everything happens for a reason even if you can't see the silver lining right now. This time will pass and you'll look back one day and realize why things had to happen the way they did.

CLOSER TO LOVE

When we break
we will never be the same again

That's because
we transform and evolve
as we piece ourselves
back together

CLOSER TO LOVE

It's okay if
you don't understand yet
but you will
that day is coming
be gentle with yourself
you're still learning

— We all are —

Remembering

CLOSER TO LOVE

I am not here for me
I am here for we

For humanity
and my family tree

To set myself and them

— *Free*

and the more I believe this
the more I perceive

CLOSER TO LOVE

I am a soul in a human's body
who has lived many lifetimes before this one
I'm not quite human
and I'm not originally from here
I'm just visiting

I'm here to help with the planetary ascension
to anchor in the new earth
and shift the old paradigm into the new

Chances are
if you are reading this
so are you

We are a part of something greater
Let's change the world together

CLOSER TO LOVE

Welcome to my alternate reality

— You are now entering the space ship —

Aka — *my mind*

CLOSER TO LOVE

Society left me feeling caged
wing clipped in a zoo

I've decided I'm no longer going to live life
the way they expect me to

A muse for someone else's entertainment

I no longer want to be enclosed
in this controlled containment

I've decided I am going to escape the nest of this world
and break the mold

I wasn't ever meant to be caged
or put into a hold

— I was born to be free …
… and so were you —

CLOSER TO LOVE

I'll take off my mask

if you take off yours

CLOSER TO LOVE

What if life is just a dream

that we are sleep walking through?

CLOSER TO LOVE

The universe doesn't apologize
for its **depth**
or all the empty s p a c e
it fills

Therefore
why should I?

CLOSER TO LOVE

She ignites a fiery path
wherever she goes

Like a struck match
being thrown to gasoline

She burns fiercely and brightly

— *Blazing*

CLOSER TO LOVE

She is exotic and expansive
like the things she craves

The oceans
The mountains
The hidden depths of nature
The stars
The universe

She is drawn to these things because she sees a
piece of herself in them
She carries a vast mystery within
where she remains hidden and unknown to herself
So she can relate to their mysteriousness

She is a galaxy
an entire world of her own

CLOSER TO LOVE

Whenever I'm feeling lost
I just tap into the codes within my soul

Home is what's within
— *ET phone home*

CLOSER TO LOVE

She doesn't think in black and white

                but all the shades in between

CLOSER TO LOVE

We are one spec
in this vast multiverse

one drop in the ocean

CLOSER TO LOVE

I'm not meant to fit into anyones box except my own
I'm not here to help others understand me
I'm here to understand myself

— *Innerstand* —

CLOSER TO LOVE

I do not fear death
because I think of death as a
further exploration of the soul

The journey does not end
instead
it keeps going

Like, moving from one state of consciousness
realm or dimension
into another

Death to me is not an end sentence
Its much more like a portal

Leaving this form of existence
or consciousness
and entering something *new*

CLOSER TO LOVE

In a quantum field of energy
shifting between dimensions
and alternate realities
she is a multi-dimensional being
existing on all planes of existence
simultaneously

CLOSER TO LOVE

It gets a little noisy inside my mind
it's like a web browser
with 50 tabs open at a time

— *Other thinking*

CLOSER TO LOVE

Slowly

    tiptoeing

        away from reality

and into

my mind

    — *Safe*

CLOSER TO LOVE

                              I am a time traveler

                         A tourist to my past and future

CLOSER TO LOVE

Funny thing about thoughts
... they don't always make sense

Kinda like this phenomena
we call life

CLOSER TO LOVE

When I can't sleep at night
I close my eyes and imagine myself
lying underneath the night sky

Instead of counting sheep
I count the stars
as they shoot across the sky

CLOSER TO LOVE

The trees wave at me
as they bend — sway

in the wind

CLOSER TO LOVE

My head is always
whirling around in outer space
... Dreaming

Sometimes it's a curse
and other times
it's the perfect antidote
from the chaos
in this world

Nonetheless ...
I long to be back in the stars

CLOSER TO LOVE

When my soul sister and I were talking on the phone with each other one late summer evening, I asked her to step outside and look up at the stars. Once she was looking, I told her to look at the middle star of Orion's Belt and then we could both be looking at the same star in the sky at the same time. I told her I had my hand over my heart and in that same moment, we both sent each other love telepathically.

It was one of those cosmic moments. The kind of moment that melts into your psyche and leaves a mark on you. I won't ever forget this night. The details will forever be etched into my memory.

Although we were states away with hundreds of miles between us, I couldn't have felt closer. She is a part of my galactic family.

— *Someone special*

CLOSER TO LOVE

I always want to know
what's going on within peoples' minds
and what they are thinking about

Maybe that's because secretly
I want others to be curious enough
to know what goes on within mine

CLOSER TO LOVE

The fog rolled off of the lake
to our feet
at the water's edge

Behind it
exposing the colors of the trees
where autumn is about to breathe her last breath
into the next season

As the clouds move by
they expose the sunrise
and for once
life was moving clockwise

This motion picture film is drawing me in
and all I can think about is
how I get to witness something so beautiful
and get to share this with him

As my father gazed into the sun
I faced him
the color amber exposed
in the shadows of his brown eyes

CLOSER TO LOVE

I felt like I actually saw him
basking on the edge
of the window to his soul

The sound of the leaves danced in the wind
with some rustling and fluttering to the ground ...

On the inside
I smiled
trying to take this moment in
and let it leave a mark on me

Knowing this moment
would be the turning of a new leaf

— *new beginnings ...*

... re-writing a timeline —

CLOSER TO LOVE

I'm not interested in surface level things. Everything I do and enjoy, has depth and great meaning.

Have you ever thought that even after someone tells you everything about themselves, there is always more to know and I can about guarantee there will always be something someone will hold back.

It's impossible to know everything and that's what intrigues me. I want to know the parts of people that they are afraid to display to the world. *I desire to be deeply intimate.*

CLOSER TO LOVE

When I looked through the gateway
of her eyes and into her soul
I began to cry
because I recognized the sadness
she hid so well behind them
I wanted to take away her pain
and replace it with the love
she so greatly deserved

— *Mí familia*

CLOSER TO LOVE

I've always found people fascinating
I've always enjoyed learning about others and
observing the details that make them up of who they are
What separates them from the rest of everyone else
and what truly makes them unique

Because not two people are made entirely the same

CLOSER TO LOVE

I am

    like an astronaut

        and people

        are like galaxies

I have yet

    to explore

CLOSER TO LOVE

Sometimes I need to disappear
and break free for awhile
to let my free spirit soar

Sometimes I get sucked into the matrix
a little too much and I need to unplug
and find my way back to my roots

Away from civilization
and the concrete jungle

To remind myself and rediscover
the blue prints and the whispers of life
that are embedded into the universe

CLOSER TO LOVE

When I'm lost or confused
I stare off into the darkened sky
and as the universe guides me home
my ego melts away from me and into

the abyss

— o —

CLOSER TO LOVE

Mother Nature offers a canopy

to all of those wild souls who feel lost

CLOSER TO LOVE

There is something peaceful and settling
about waking up with the sun

When everything is still slightly at a stand still
just before the slow of traffic begins

CLOSER TO LOVE

The lights

        danced and carved themselves

in and out of the night sky

        leaving a trace of cut colors

— *Northern Lights*

CLOSER TO LOVE

From a young age
I was always trying to find a way
to connect with nature

From climbing trees and chasing birds
to making shapes out of clouds that would float by
or laying under the stars and counting them
as they would shoot across the sky

I still enjoy wiggling my toes
in the grass and sand
Even as an adult
I still wonder if this whole time

Earth was *Neverland*

CLOSER TO LOVE

When I was driving down the road
in the middle of summer
both sides of it were lined
with an abundance of wildflowers
and for a moment
I thought I was on my way to

heaven

CLOSER TO LOVE

Talk to the animals
Feel the elements of water
earth, fire and air
Smile with the sun
moon
and stars
Look at them with
wonder and admiration
Smell the flowers and hug the trees
Put your feet on the Earth's surface
and just be

— *Ground yourself*

CLOSER TO LOVE

Oh how I've missed you mother ocean
and dancing in the heart of your waves
Your smiling waters drive me wild
and put me into a daze

Beneath your waves
lies my heart
We are connected
never apart

Visiting you is like seeing
a long lost friend
I wish our time together
never had to end

Once again
you've swept me off my feet
and carried away my soul
You are one of the only things
that makes this vast soul of mine

Entirely whole

CLOSER TO LOVE

I've never truly known why
my heart is drawn to the ocean so much
It started out as an obsession
It is all consuming
wild...
You can see its beginning
but not its end

Rarely placid
sometimes raging
It's incomprehensible
filled with adventure
exposing a whole new world beneath its surface

CLOSER TO LOVE

Sit outside in nature with a journal
Observe your surroundings
What do you see and how does it make you feel?

Do a check in

Hows life?
Whats going good?
What are you loving?
Whats real?
What are you thankful for?

And watch the magic that unfolds

CLOSER TO LOVE

The stillness in nature

    gives me the answers I seek

CLOSER TO LOVE

I have come to the conclusion

that I trust animals and nature

more than I trust most humans

CLOSER TO LOVE

Follow your magic
and it will not lead you astray
The only thing that will
is if fear makes you stay

It can be hard when your heart
has an unquenchable thirst
Following your dreams
can be scary at first
But what could be worse?

Other than doing something
for the rest of your life
that you'll deeply regret

It can be intimidating
never fully knowing what
faith

will make you do next

CLOSER TO LOVE

The people who follow their dreams
generally aren't realists

They are wild
crazy and
curious

CLOSER TO LOVE

I like harmony
with everything

music
relationships
life

When everything is in sync
and flows
beautifully

CLOSER TO LOVE

She was an

incurable romantic

weaving

    her passions

into reality

CLOSER TO LOVE

To crack the code
one must dive deep
into the trenches
of their soul

To understand
one must go
within themselves

CLOSER TO LOVE

The universe leaves a little bread crumb trail
for those who are willing to follow

It has the answers
for those who listen

CLOSER TO LOVE

Come with me

    I will help you

wake up

    from this dream

Becoming

CLOSER TO LOVE

Laying in your arms caress
I grab your hands and
pull them close to my chest
I begin to fall into a dream about
the stars and how they align
Just like our souls and
how they are intertwined

How did we come about to be?

CLOSER TO LOVE

Sometimes moments

    speak for themselves

        and words

            aren't necessary

CLOSER TO LOVE

A life without you
is like plucking rays of light
from the sun
slowly
the days become much colder
and darker

CLOSER TO LOVE

The way she pulls her hair

    out of a messy bun

        tumbling down and out

like small cresting waves

    whispering over her shoulders

        and down the small of her back

—*Hair for days*

CLOSER TO LOVE

Her love was like a bolt of lightning
a defibrillator upon their hearts
and bringing their sleeping souls
back to life

— *Revive & Awaken*

CLOSER TO LOVE

When the sun fell behind the horizon
and the moon came out
so did her inner wild woman

CLOSER TO LOVE

At night

in the middle of my dreams

my heart reaches for you

CLOSER TO LOVE

In the quiet wake that resides between us
there is proof
that you can still love
in silence

To love — *telepathically*

CLOSER TO LOVE

I went to the doctor
but all they said was,
"I'm sorry, it's just … there's no remedy
for an incurable romantic."

… Well …
that's fucking great

I have stage four love cancer
and it'll surely be the death of me

— *Love is infectious*

CLOSER TO LOVE

Heart: "Is it safe?"

Brain: "No."

Heart: "Alright, I'm gonna do it anyway."

Brain: "…"

CLOSER TO LOVE

His love poured out of him and into her
just like God poured the stars into the night sky

The love they share is radiant

Even in the darkest nights
their love always shines

CLOSER TO LOVE

A soothing love

calms the fiery soul

CLOSER TO LOVE

You are like the S u N
that shines on my life

A F i R e
that brightens my heart
and W a R m S my soul

CLOSER TO LOVE

A hug
is a gesture that speaks
when words can not

CLOSER TO LOVE

A love that is longing

is not easily filled

CLOSER TO LOVE

Getting naked to me ...

is letting someone
undress
my mind

CLOSER TO LOVE

Their hearts melted into each other
like a marshmallow into chocolate

Give me S'more of that love

CLOSER TO LOVE

She could easily narrate an 'R' rated film
with the thoughts she has for him

—Parental advisory, Explicit content

CLOSER TO LOVE

Every time I gaze into his eyes
I get lost in their depths

Like a sailor exploring the seas
without a sense of direction

CLOSER TO LOVE

> He's a mystery
> to my brain
>
> but my heart
> understands him fully

CLOSER TO LOVE

Love is like a fire
and if it is fed and nourished
it could burn forever
but if it is starved
watch it slowly fade away

A fiery love that
B u R n S
requires mindfulness
dedication
and work

A F i E r Y passionate love
hardly burns on its own

CLOSER TO LOVE

His love

was like the steady flow

of a current

CLOSER TO LOVE

In him
holds the missing fragments
of my soul

— *Divine counterpart*

CLOSER TO LOVE

He looked at her and said

You're just like fine whiskey

The more you age
the better you taste
and the more beautiful
you become

CLOSER TO LOVE

She wanted a love
that watered her
nurtured her
and helped her grow

Just like the sun and rain
that gives life to the flowers
in spring

CLOSER TO LOVE

Be with someone
who is willing to undress you

Not just physically
but mentally
emotionally
and spiritually

To pull all your layers back
one by one

until there are no more layers left
and they are just left there
to the very core of you

Completely naked

CLOSER TO LOVE

You deserve someone who does
all the little things

It's the smaller gestures
that make up everything big

CLOSER TO LOVE

You are a desirable person
everything about you

Someone will love you
the way you deserve to be loved
some day

Rising

You are love incarnate
Remember

CLOSER TO LOVE

In a world of illusions
she tends to disconnect
and disappear from "reality"
in order to relocate herself

lost 'n found

CLOSER TO LOVE

Reaching higher

Searching deeper

Looking further

CLOSER TO LOVE

Who you are meant to be
is who you always were

… it's there …

Buried within you

CLOSER TO LOVE

The things that you perceive
aren't always true

Question everything

— *always*

CLOSER TO LOVE

See beyond the veils
of this realm

CLOSER TO LOVE

Like a diamond
you are multi-faceted

You are a multi-dimensional being
with many different aspects of
who you were
who you are
and who you are yet to be

You are
I am

CLOSER TO LOVE

There are some things your soul won't let you forget
Like how you came into this plane of existence
with a sense of inner knowing

That there is something more

beyond us
—

CLOSER TO LOVE

The same God that breathed life
into the stars
and the universe

also breathed life
and resides within
me and you

We are one

CLOSER TO LOVE

What you believe your mission is
What you believe you came here to be a part of
What you believe you came here to be

— It's all real —

If you think it ...
 ... it is —

CLOSER TO LOVE

You can be anything you want to be
You can do anything you want to do

and it all starts with the belief that

you can —

CLOSER TO LOVE

— Remember —
Remember who you are
Remember your truth
Remember your purpose
Remember your heart
Remember your soul
Come back home
To the pillowy cushion of your heart

— Remember —

CLOSER TO LOVE

I am just a different version of you
and you are just a different version of me

We are different
yet
we are the same

CLOSER TO LOVE

I wish you could see yourself
through the eyes
of those who

love you

CLOSER TO LOVE

To judge yourself

is to judge the source
that created you

CLOSER TO LOVE

— When you're judging others, you're really just judging yourself —

If you find you're having strong opinions and judgments toward others, look at where in your life you judge or have strong opinions towards yourself.

The more critical we are toward ourselves, the more we tend to project that onto others. When we approach things with neutrality rather than duality and polarity we release ourselves from judgment.

How we see and treat ourselves is generally how we see and treat others. We are each other's mirrors.

How you treat others says a lot about you
How they treat you says a lot about them.

CLOSER TO LOVE

Gentle
Loving
Fierce
Affectionate
Nurturing
Safe
Strong
Powerful
Beautiful

You are everything
and everything is you

CLOSER TO LOVE

No matter how hard I try
I can't quite drown out the whispers of my heart
it's always encouraging me

to share more love

— always —

CLOSER TO LOVE

curiosity of

l o v e

outweighs the risk of

p a i n

CLOSER TO LOVE

You don't have to hide who you are
when you're around me
I won't judge you
I will accept you
and love you
fully

— your heart no longer needs to go unseen

CLOSER TO LOVE

When you focus on the things you love about yourself
you'll find yourself focusing on the things you love
about everyone else

When you change your perception towards yourself
and heal what's within you
it'll change your external reality
and the way you view life

Everyone and everything

— *The shift*

CLOSER TO LOVE

Love is there
if you look for it

Light is there
if you look for it

Goodness is there
if you look for it

: It requires mindful focus :

All you have to do is

— Notice —

CLOSER TO LOVE

How you love yourself
sets the standard
for how others will

love you

CLOSER TO LOVE

When we are struggling
we need to get in the habit of asking ourselves,

"How can I love myself more during this time?"

CLOSER TO LOVE

When we love ourselves unconditionally
we are able to love others unconditionally
and we see life through the eyes of love more

The more we love ourselves
the more love we are able to give to others

CLOSER TO LOVE

When we feel better about ourselves
we feel better about other people too
and wanting to do good

This is why learning how to love ourselves from the inside out is so important and one of the factors in how we will change and heal the planet.

If we want to take better care of the planet then we need to learn how to take better care of ourselves.

CLOSER TO LOVE

Recall the missing fragments
of your soul
Retrieve what has been lost
in order for you to

— *Remember*

CLOSER TO LOVE

Unconditional love doesn't know any boundaries
It melts through judgment and illusion
It allows people to truly be seen
Beyond the choices we make or mistakes we have made
It is all knowing and understanding
that we all have experienced sadness
hurt, anger and pain

Love sees through polarity and is neutral
Love is what sets us free

The people that are hurt
just need more love

Love from others
from self
and mostly
love from God

Give people a chance
Look beyond their choices and truly see them
Try to understand

We are all in this life together

Think of a time when you needed more love
and be that for others

love can never be wrong

CLOSER TO LOVE

We are all created from the same source
We aren't that different from each other

The matrix has fueled disconnection
and separation between us for years
but we don't need to allow that
We can be rebels with a cause
and fight against it

For humanity
For freedom
For harmony
For unity
For the collective
… For Love …

There is no room for separation
if we are to rise

— Are you feelin' it now Mr. Krabz?

CLOSER TO LOVE

Make it a priority to purposefully search
for something beautiful in someone

Even the people that hurt you
or are unkind to you

Show them how to love

CLOSER TO LOVE

Divided people are easy to rule and take over
but united people are not

At what point have we grown so disconnected from each other?

It is time to come out of the dark
and step into the light

Like the sun

together
we will
rise

— *Unity in totality*

CLOSER TO LOVE

Protecting the values of balance
peace, unity, love and harmony

— *Guardian of the Lemurian Codes*

CLOSER TO LOVE

Just like a rose

You are
beautiful

Thorns and all

CLOSER TO LOVE

Something just clicked for me over the last couple of years that made me question, "What the fuck am I doing?"
That is exactly the conversation that I had with myself.

Why did I cover myself up, thinking that was the best thing? From being true to me? Why did I allow peoples comments, judgments, thoughts and projections define who I am/was? Why did I internalize their interpretation of me or projection of themselves? Why couldn't I be the me that I am when I'm alone? Why was I giving people power over my life? Why did I live in fear and give people the power to judge me?

In the end, it doesn't even matter what people think of me.

Whether or not I had approval from others.
Whether people liked me.
What I wore.
What I had.

None of it would've mattered.

I no longer trust the small thinking of others.

CLOSER TO LOVE

>Who I am now
>is who I was
>all along
>
>I remembered
>I didn't lose myself
>to this world
>
>— *the red pill*

CLOSER TO LOVE

To worry about others rejecting you
is to reject yourself

I started to become more of myself around people
when I stopped fearing rejection

Because I understand that I can't lose
what is truly meant for me
and if I do lose people for being myself
then there is something better coming

CLOSER TO LOVE

Let's be vulnerable
hearts wide open

Tell me what lights up your soul
Tell me what makes your heart bleed
Tell me what makes you feel whole
Tell me about the happiest day of your life
Tell me about your hopes and dreams
Tell me about your fears
Tell me about the last time you cried
because something was so captivatingly beautiful
Tell me about the times
that you wish never ended
Tell me about the people you love
and why you love
Tell me about the time when you
felt so strongly about something
that it shook you to the core

I want to feel you

So please
do tell

CLOSER TO LOVE

Visualize yourself as a magnet

    being pulled towards all the things

                  that you feel worthy of

CLOSER TO LOVE

Affirm:

I will not be defined by my past
I do not allow my past to have power over me
My past is a tool that has helped me to get to where I am today
I would not be who I am today without yesterday

I am grateful
for my misfortunes
because I understand that they are a teacher to me
I forgive others and myself because I can not rewrite
what has been done

Today my past does not hold power over me
or keep me from having peace in this present moment
Today I choose to love myself
others
and release myself
from the past

Today I choose to forgive myself
and those that have hurt me
to set them and myself free

Don't let the past
weigh you down

Let go

CLOSER TO LOVE

You gotta bring it to love

That part of yourself you can't seem to forgive?
Bring it to love
That part of yourself that makes you angry?
Bring it to love
That part of yourself that you struggle to accept?
Bring it to love
When you're sad or depressed?
Bring it to love

Another words,
everything you are experiencing . . .

Shine some light on it and
bring it to love

CLOSER TO LOVE

What happened yesterday
is not who you are today

Don't identify yourself with someone
you no longer are

CLOSER TO LOVE

— *Worry* —

How much of what weighs you down, is not yours to carry?

Instead of worrying about things you can't control, like the choices others make or the way others behave, devote that energy into something more productive.

When thoughts and moments of doubt come, notice it and let it go immediately. Replace it with a positive affirmation.

You are not your fears.
You are not your worries.
You are not your anxiety.

Think about the things you want rather than the things you're afraid of.

Think of all the ways that something could go right.
Think of all the reasons it will work and what you have to gain.

CLOSER TO LOVE

Just for a moment
pretend that fear doesn't exist
as if you weren't attached to your own insecurities

Step outside of body and look at yourself

What do you see?
What do you think?

The reason why people can see the good things in you
your beauty
and your talents
is because they aren't attached to your fears
insecurities and limiting self beliefs

See the good things that people see in you
and believe that they are true

CLOSER TO LOVE

Do me a favor and look at the you from a few years ago

How are you different?
In which areas have you grown?
Would your past self look up to your present self?

Use yourself as your own inspiration

My goal is to only be a better me tomorrow
than I am today

and a better me today
than I was yesterday

CLOSER TO LOVE

There is something in your life that you're wanting
something that maybe you don't have ... yet

Slow down and sink into your heart

What do you have right now that you can be grateful for?

The more we express gratitude
we interrupt thoughts of anxiousness and negativity

Whenever I need to get out of my headspace
and more into my heart

I express gratitude
even for the things I don't have yet

— Believe in the good things that are coming your way

CLOSER TO LOVE

Mindfulness is asking yourself:

What do I have right now to be grateful for?
What do I have right now to love?
What is going good for me right now?
What do I have to appreciate?
What is beautiful about life right now?

When you do this, you are switching your mindset and your frequency to serve you in the now. Whenever you find your mind wandering to the past or future, reel it back into the now and ask yourself those questions. ^^^

Practicing mindfulness has changed my life.
It made me realize how much beauty truly surrounds me in every moment. There are every day things that are just waiting to be noticed. There is magic all around us. All we need to do is pause and tune in.

The trees leaves blowing in the breeze
a butterfly crossing my path
or an eagle soaring above
all whispering….

See me
Notice me
Inviting me

into the present moment

CLOSER TO LOVE

You are an amazing human being
who loves
cares
and nurtures
deeply

You are strong
and can accomplish anything
you set yourself out to be

Giving up is not an option
Keep fighting
Keep showing up
and remember your why

You'll get there soon
even if it doesn't feel that way now

You are worthy of your hearts greatest desires
You deserve what your soul craves

I love you
You have come so far
Keep going
Don't give up
I believe in you

CLOSER TO LOVE

Think of yourself as Peter Pan
with a little bit of pixie dust

You already have wings
you just need to believe

—*you can fly*

CLOSER TO LOVE

Even when others don't seem to notice
appreciate or validate you
be those things to yourself

Notice your growth and expansion
Notice yourself and how far you have come
and the battles you have faced

Appreciate who you are and what you have to offer
Appreciate everything there is to love about you
Focus on your positive qualities and enhancing them more
Validate yourself and be proud of who you are

Who you are now
and who you are still becoming

CLOSER TO LOVE

If you feel like you are lacking support
where in your life are you not supporting yourself?

If you feel like you are lacking love
where in your life are you not loving yourself?

If you feel like no one cares about you
where in your life are you not caring enough
about yourself?

Our feelings, emotions and inner dialogue
are an invitation from our bodies

Telling us that there is an area within that we are
neglecting and that we need to pay a little more close
attention to

Spend time with yourself
Get in-tune with yourself and your heart

Your soul is always speaking

CLOSER TO LOVE

Generally the things we need from other people
are the things we need to be giving to ourselves

CLOSER TO LOVE

Be courageous enough
to speak your truth
so you can invite others
to be brave enough to do the same

to be seen
to be felt
to be heard

Speak your truth

CLOSER TO LOVE

Affirm:

I reclaim my power
I am expressive
I speak my truth

CLOSER TO LOVE

I'm here to remind you today
that you are a powerful being

You have the power
to create any reality you want

You have the power
to over come any obstacle thrown your way

You have the power to rise
even when it can feel a lot like falling at first

— *You are powerful*

CLOSER TO LOVE

Thank your troubles that you are facing

because something good is about to come out of them

CLOSER TO LOVE

You don't always have to attach a reason
as to why you are feeling emotional

Just let it pass through you

Do not fight your emotions

Witness them

Observe your feelings
without judgment

CLOSER TO LOVE

— Embrace your own uniqueness —

My whole life I always wanted to fit in
and now I've learned to embrace everything that makes
me different

I no longer wish to fit in
because that would imply that I'm just like everyone else

I would only be doing myself and the world a disservice
by denying my own uniqueness

You were born to be you
not like someone else

CLOSER TO LOVE

Suppressing who I was
came with a heavy burden

Being true to myself
is something I'm still learning

CLOSER TO LOVE

Don't give so much off of your plate
until there is nothing left for yourself

This is not how you sacrifice love

If you don't set boundaries and save some love for yourself
people will take and take until there is nothing left

Who would still love you and be around if you said *"no?"*

CLOSER TO LOVE

You don't need to prove yourself to anyone
Give yourself the approval you seek from others

You are good enough for you
You don't owe anyone an explanation

CLOSER TO LOVE

People's opinions of you

become irrelevant

when you learn to accept yourself

for who you are

rather than seeking approval

from others

CLOSER TO LOVE

Be the friend that you are to everyone else

with yourself

CLOSER TO LOVE

Make sure you are treating yourself
the way you want others to treat you

CLOSER TO LOVE

Believe what your heart tells you
not what others say
No matter what you do or how hard you try
there will always be those with strong opinions
who think they know what's best for you

Stay grounded in your values
and stand confident in who you are

The darkness always fights the hardest
when it knows God has something great in store for you

CLOSER TO LOVE

Don't shrink yourself down
to fit in

Don't be afraid
of your truth

Don't be afraid
of the power you hold within

CLOSER TO LOVE

Here's what I do know:

You deserve the greatest love
You deserve the freedom of self expression
and to be who you are

If your self expression is off putting to someone else
you know there is an issue

Not with you
with them

Don't stop being yourself
because someone else doesn't like it

People only see you through their own perception
and where they are at with their own personal journey

Hell, they could be triggered because
maybe deep down they want to be themselves too
but have not yet healed themselves
and over come their own fears

Keep showing up
Keep shining like you do

CLOSER TO LOVE

What are the people in your life like?
The ones that you spend the most time with?

Did you know that we are the company we keep?
We tend to mirror characteristics of the top five people
we spend the most time with

So let me ask you
are the people you are spending time with
in alignment with where you want to see yourself
your mission
and where you're going?

How do your people show up for you?
What do you want and look for in your relationships with
people? Are the people in your life loving and supportive?
Are they respectful and caring?

CLOSER TO LOVE

If you are finding that people aren't in alignment with
your needs then it's time to evaluate and ask yourself
why you are still hanging on

This is an act of self love

If you are still engaging with toxic relationships
you will attract more of that in your life
because that is what you're choosing to settle with

If you don't like the way people treat you
let go and move on so God can create space for those
that will meet your standards

CLOSER TO LOVE

You are not responsible
for the way others see you

You are only responsible
for the way you
see yourself

CLOSER TO LOVE

Let them judge you
Let them misunderstand you
Let them gossip about you

Their opinions aren't your problem
You stay kind, committed to love and free in your authenticity

No matter what they do or say
don't you dare doubt your worth

Just keep shining like you do

Don't be afraid of losing people

Be afraid of losing yourself trying to please everyone around you

CLOSER TO LOVE

If humans struggle to be kind to you
just see them as needing more love

CLOSER TO LOVE

It's your choice.

You get to choose who is in your life and if you don't like the way people treat you or act, you don't have to compromise yourself. If you continuously let people in your life that don't value you or that are toxic, your life won't change. Personally, I would rather be alone than engage with toxicity. If it doesn't resonate with you and your energetic signature, send them back to God with love. It doesn't mean that anyone is a "bad" person.

Choose to engage with those that will love, encourage, support and respect you and challenge you to grow and reach your highest potential. Always trust what feels right. The right people in your life, will make you feel good and feel loved.

Pay attention to the people you are with when you feel loved and accepted for who you are. Those are the ones to hang onto.

Always go with what feels right.

CLOSER TO LOVE

Growth = Change

Don't focus on what you have to lose
Focus on what you have to gain

CLOSER TO LOVE

Every time you find yourself
wishing for things that haven't happened yet

let it go

Turn to what is in this moment
and focus on what makes you feel abundant now

CLOSER TO LOVE

Affirm:

The faster I let go of the resistance of things

The faster I am able to manifest change

— Surrender to the flow

CLOSER TO LOVE

It is time
To rise as a collective
To step out of fear
and into love

To remember who we are

We are all an extension of cosmic creation
Divine energy circulates through all of us
The same spark that was used to create life
is within all of us

We have all felt love
We have all felt pain
We have all suffered from something

CLOSER TO LOVE

We aren't that different from each other
We need to stop furthering the divide between us
By coming together
To love ourselves and one another
To accept ourselves and one another
To create harmony and peace with ourselves and with each other

To see life through the eyes of love more

We need to focus on what connects us
rather than what separates us

— *If we are to rise*

CLOSER TO LOVE

I laid in the moon kissed grass one late summer evening
and starred up and into the night sky at the stars

when a soft and gentle voice whispered to my heart
"Do you see how it is all connected?"

With tears of awe
slowly falling down my face
and melting into my cheeks

I whispered back to the universe

Yes
I see

I Innerstand

CLOSER TO LOVE

Source is the breath we connect to
and the air around us

Source is infinite
everywhere and in everything

In all creation
ourselves
and each other

Spirit's signature is left on everything
seen and unseen

We are all connected
We are all one large intricate web of life

CLOSER TO LOVE

You

are

an

expression

of

light

and

love

Afterword

My hope for you is that no matter what happens in this life, that you never forget your heart. That you never lose sense of who you are, your essence or lose your gentler self. Things get really hard in life sometimes, things that try to snuff out our light. It's easy to get caught up in working, our responsibilities and internalizing all the things that people say to us, about us or do to us. This is not you. To your core, you are who you set yourself out to be.

Always bring it back to your heart and the true essence of your being.

Never forget, always remember.

This is for you

this is for me

I wouldn't be

without you

I love you

I see you

Thank you

About the Author

Jena Rose is an Aries (sun), Sagittarius (moon) and Leo (rising); an INFJ-A and Enneagram type 4. She is an intuitive, self-published writer and author of two collections of poetry, quotes and prose. Her works include *Entangled by Nature* and *Closer to Love*. She is a mental health counselor, a multi-dimensional energy worker, modern mystic, self-taught artist, a medicine woman and spiritual teacher working as an integration guide for others. Jena is an aura reader and owner of Aurora Aura. She also works with healing instruments such as singing bowls and offers sound therapy, healing transmissions along with other ceremonial offerings as a way to help navigate others within themselves.

Jena's fascination with consciousness, energy, and the metaphysical/spiritual world began at a really young age. It was almost like she was called to do this work from the very beginning. Even when she was a little girl, her deepest desire was to change the world and she has always been drawn to the things, 'unseen.' As time went on there were many synchronicities that lined up that continued to pull her more into this calling. She has experienced many spontaneous awakenings throughout her lifetime that have only deepened her consciousness and self awareness. The more she began to gain awareness of a deeper love and universal consciousness, that was when the idea of *Closer to Love* was born, along with many other cosmic things.

Author's Note

As a collective, we heal and connect through love and maybe if we can all find that love from within, then we will be able to love without and thus, change the world. Through the act of love and consciousness.

The only way to change the world is to first change the world within us. We do this by having a desire to take care of ourselves and to truly love ourselves within. Once this is achieved, we are then able to share that with the rest of the world. Like a ripple effect, we will echo love so that others may do the same.

Love,
—*Jena Rose*

www.ingramcontent.com/pod-product-compliance
Lightning Source LLC
Chambersburg PA
CBHW022049290426
44109CB00014B/1032

Author's Note

As a collective, we heal and connect through love and maybe if we can all find that love from within, then we will be able to love without and thus, change the world. Through the act of love and consciousness.

The only way to change the world is to first change the world within us. We do this by having a desire to take care of ourselves and to truly love ourselves within. Once this is achieved, we are then able to share that with the rest of the world. Like a ripple effect, we will echo love so that others may do the same.

Love,
—*Jena Rose*

www.ingramcontent.com/pod-product-compliance
Lightning Source LLC
Chambersburg PA
CBHW022049290426
44109CB00014B/1032